Zurich

Ella and Bella go to Zürich by Bobby I.K.

Illustrations by Bella Maher
Edited by Meghan Helms

First edition

"TO MY LOVELY FAMILY"

Ella and Bella are two adorable sisters. They love to travel and now they are about to set out on one of the most exciting journeys of their lives. Many adventures await them in one of the most beautiful countries in the world, Switzerland. Their Daddy has just gotten an interesting new job in **Zürich**, the biggest city in **Switzerland**, so whole family is moving there.

The family is packing their bags and getting ready for their exciting trip.

"Do we really have to move?" Ella asks.

"Honey, many adventures and new friends await you there!" Mummy explains.

"In that case, we can't wait for these adventures to begin!" Ella laughs happily.

"Sweetie, do you need all that stuff?" Mummy asks Bella.

"Yes, especially the **toys!**"

"Mummy, I'm a bit scared of flying on a plane!" Bella says quietly. She doesn't want Ella to hear her.

"There is nothing to be afraid of, sweetheart! It's always fun to fly on a plane. You can see the whole world from high above and look down on the mountains and cities!" Mummy tells her.

When they first get on the plane, Ella and Bella are so excited about the trip that they can't stop laughing and talking over each other. Soon, however, they lose interest and become bored.

"When will we get there?" Ella asks.

"Are we close?" asks Bella.

"We are still a ways away, girls. Instead of asking me if we are there every other minute, how about you two play a game to help pass the time," Mummy suggests.

"Let's imagine that clouds are different animals and make up stories with them!" Ella suggests.

"Great idea!" says Bella.

Off they fly, higher and higher above the clouds. A few hours later, their pilot makes an announcement: "We are about to land in **Zürich, Switzerland!**"

Mummy and Daddy make a promise to take the girls on a sightseeing tour in Zürich and to go see the **Zoo** which is one of the largest in **Europe.** Of course, they won't miss a visit the **Lindt** chocolate museum too. They will go to **Rhine Falls** as well, one of the most impressive waterfalls in the world.

The next day, Ella and Bella wake up early, impatiently waiting for the day's adventure to begin. The whole family goes for a walk around the picturesque and charming Zürich old town. The beautiful and historic **Grossmünster Cathedral** towers over this part of the city near the **Limmat river.**

The girls crane their necks to take in the impressive monument.

"Kids, do you want to go inside the cathedral and take a look?" Daddy asks.
"Yes, but another time! We want to have a ride on the **carousel**," Ella replies impatiently.

Of course, Ella and Bella take a ride!
The girls enjoy a turn on this
beautifully restored vintage carousel
riding on horses with colorful manes.
"It looks like it came out of a
fairytale!" Ella happily shouts.

Later on, the family head to one of the symbols of Zurich, the nostalgic **Polybahn.** It links the old town with a beautiful viewing terraces high above the city. The panorama terrace is located in front of the main building of the Federal Institute of Technology. "This is one of the best universities in the world, kids! I hope that one day you will study here! Did you know that **Albert Einstein** studied in here? He was awarded the **Nobel Prize,"** Daddy enthusiastically explains.

The family strolls down to **Zürich Lake** to see the swans that live there. "Mummy, they are so beautiful. Let's feed them!" suggests Ella. "Do they turn into princesses at night as in the fairytale?" Bella curiously asks.

Mummy just smiles.

The girls play around the lake all afternoon, feeding the swan and imagining the beautiful princesses they turn into. "When can we go the zoo?" Bella asks.

The next day it is time to head to the zoo. Ella and Bella are very excited and can't wait to see all the animals. **Zürich Zoo** is one of the biggest zoos in Europe.

The girls get their little backpacks ready, filling them with their favorite animal books. "Come on in!" Ella and Bella shout as they arrive at the zoo.

"Kids, today we will be meeting **wild animals!**" Daddy says.
"Don't worry! There is nothing to be afraid of," says Mummy.
"Let's go to the **giraffes** first!" Ella and Bella shout.

The giraffes live in a savannah along with hippos and zebras. At the giraffe's feeding place, they have the unique opportunity to see the animals up close where they can even touch them. Ella and Bella will never forget the time they got to pet a giraffe.

Then they go straight to the elephants. The girls giggle and laugh as they watch the **elephants** bathe.

"They are very funny!" laughs Bella.

After lunch, they go to see the **penguins**.
"Penguins! They have such a goofy walk!"
Daddy says to the girls.

The family's last stop is at the **monkey** enclosure.
Bella loves watching the monkeys swing and play.
"They are so funny! Mummy, I want to live with the monkeys and play all day just like they do," Bella sighs.

After the zoo, the family's next stop is one of the most exciting places in Zürich for two little girls, the

Lindt Home of Chocolate.

There is a spectacular **chocolate fountain** at the factory which Ella and Bella cannot wait to taste and see.

As soon as they set foot inside the factory doors, the smell of cocoa is overwhelming.
Right in the center of the main hall is a 9-meter giant chocolate fountain. The girls have to be reminded multiple times that they are not allowed dip their fingers in it.

“Chocolate is made from Cocoa Beans,” Daddy explains as they explore the factory. “It has a long journey to take before it becomes chocolate.”

"This is the most delicious chocolate in the world!" Ella says happily.

“Girls, here is the **largest** Lindt chocolate shop in the whole **world!** Can you believe it?” Mummy exclaims.

After their delicious adventure, the family heads home where they sleep well with bellies full of chocolate. The next day, the family heads to **Rhine Falls.** Extremely powerful and beautiful, the waterfall is a true natural wonder. It is the largest waterfall in Europe. Ella and Bella are amazed by the waterfall's thundering beauty.

“These waterfalls have been around for more than 15,000 years,” Daddy explains. To get an even more magnificent view of the falls, they head over to **Schloss Laufen**, an ancient castle perched above the falls.

After exploring the castle, the family climbs aboard a boat to float along the **Rhine**, one of the major European rivers. The boat takes them up close to the thundering falls before gently floating down the river where Ella and Bella watch the riverside views pass by.

In the evening, Ella and Bella are still so excited that they **splash** in the bath making their own waterfalls and **jump** in their beds pretending they are princesses in their very own castle.

"It was a wonderful day! Where do you want to go next time?" asks Mummy. "Maybe in **Bern?** That is the **capital** city of **Switzerland.** I think some real bears live there!" Daddy laughs. "Really? I want to go and see them!" Bella shrieks. "Wonderful idea, girls! We are going to plan our next travel adventure soon. Goodnight, sweethearts!" Mummy says as she kisses them and tucks them into bed.

Stories

On the next travel adventure, Ella and Bella are heading off to explore **Canton of Bern.**

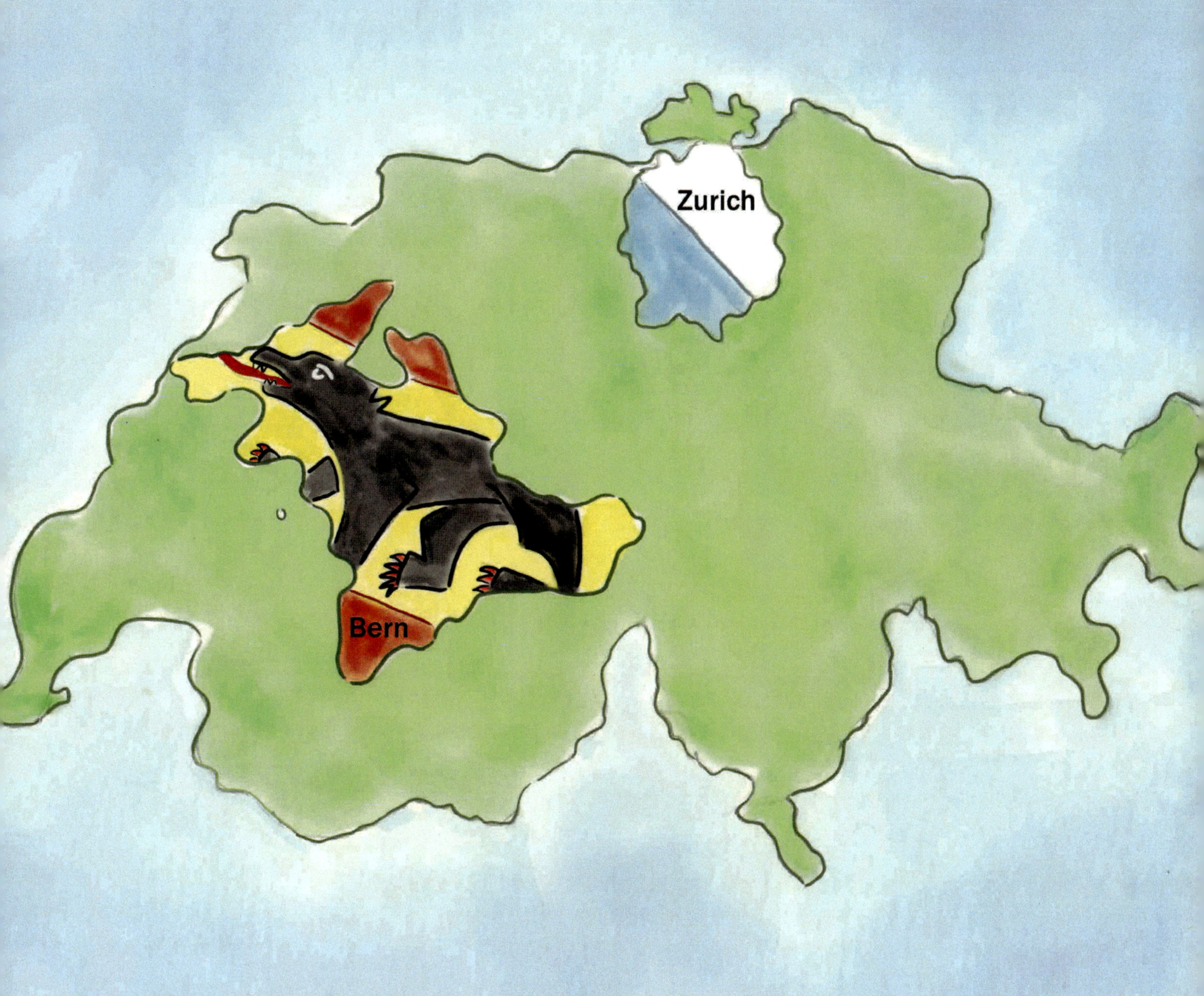
Zurich
Bern

Made in the USA
Las Vegas, NV
07 February 2024